An Artful View: Reflections on Fate

Ciarán Lloyd

For Mother,
Thank you.

CONTENTS

An Artful View

An artful view,
Looking in lieu
Of the gradations of truth.
 Lies made in jest,
Truths told in journal,
 All coming together to form

This artful view.
Mindfulness is vital
This is true of us all.
 The symbolism of you,
The criticism too,
 Combines and unites,

Forming these shades.
Colour, blues, reds,
Various hues
 In harmony
In union
 Create a portrait

Of this artful view.
Getting up close,
The personal too,
 To see the intricacies,
Of emotions and hopes, the
 Ambitions and tropes

That form you and
Conform to you
And mine to admire you.
 These eyes are disguised
You see
 To symbolise

Your artful gaze,
Your carefully crafted beauty,
Adorned with regal carvings
 Of Grecian beauty
And Roman chiseling
 That salutes your triumphant value.

The artful view,
Upon thee,
Is the touch of divinity,
 And unreal beauty
Invokes another verse
 Of tales and myths.

Yet this,
Here.
This is not alike.
 An illusion.
An insult to thee,
 An outright attack

On the fabled.
Disturbing, true,
That modern folk can see
 This disgrace of 'art'
And love it
 Nay, it is wrong.

Willfully assault it.
Cast darkness upon it,
As it flies in the face of history.
 Beauty is not as so,
Though...
 Beauty is within not the eyes

But within the essence.

As I Watch

As I watch the blood drain from me,
I wonder what I did to let hate rule me,
What lead me to pick up the blade?
I wearily wipe the crimson stains,
and sleep for several days,
and hope for hope,
but nothing comes to me.

It tortures me that this world is not for me,
Through tired eyes I see only grey and no me,
Why must I believe that it will get better?
I tempt myself to finish the task,
and sleep for several days,
and hate my hope,
but this world spins evermore, just not for me.

As I feel my body grow white, my arm goes cold,
As I wonder what pains me, grey turns red,
Why must life go on?
I fear I cannot go on,
I fear I cannot live,
I fear I cannot see at all

Blade

This, my guiding blade,
provides what I need:
fills me with relief.
Loosens the valve to
the pain of my heart.

This, my gliding blade,
slices fresh skin,
further squeezes a hollow
heart of its sin.
As an ode to hope,
though a tool for dread,
keeps me alive,
keeps me awake.

The power of pain,
held by one blade,
held by my hand,
the power to drain.

Fate

Waiting and hating,
I'm a patient patient,
slice me,
dice me,
not too late to hate me,
no self-esteem,
low valuation.
I need surgery, urgently; on my mind.
and though I admit you made me happy,
and my day was brightened,
but in every word I uttered,
my breath was frightened.
When I loved you;
I only felt degradation.

Nail me to the cross,
if you're cross with me,
feed me to the dogs,
and they bark constantly.
enslave me with chains unbreakable,
minds unalterable,
life not saveable,
speak at me with words unthinkable,
tell me you love me,
as you cut me,
I know you will leave me,
again...
But I'll come for you anyway,
so push the knife deeper,
the strife of my life is knowing that
you will be here to hear my screams,
to tear me apart at the seams whilst
my eyes tear up with broken dreams;
so scrape me up from the shattered ground,
as my empty mind smoulders with
old divine hope for love and laughter.
so what happens after we depart?
a blade of life soaring above open scars,
as I fall to my fate... but not into your arms.

Familiar

I see your face in many crowds,
And yet,
Should I see my own: it would not be
familiar.
Though many crowds contain any faces,
Non are as pure as yours.
And though I know many faces,
Non are as alluring as yours..

This is my enigma, there is no familiarity.
No one is the same,
And yet in a crowd all the faces blend.
A sea of faces becomes one wave, and though I scan each droplet of water,
None are as pure or as good or as fine as yours.
And when those droplets come to freeze or boil, I cannot be sure if
Yours, or mine, will conjoin. Though I hope it will.
And when those droplets come to thaw, will we remain as one, or will we
deform?
I cannot be sure, though I hope we won't.

And of those faces in the crowd,
Each feature: each breath, each passing
Thought, each tear; they all combine to create that face and to create that
image.
Which becomes that droplet, which becomes that wave, which becomes
that body of water.

And yet non is as pure, or as good, or as fine, as yours.

Maneuver

The silent ailment maneuvers a gentle
wave,
A whisper of the end, upon a light breeze.
An internal storm,
Seemingly peaceful.
Those who speak false truths,
They call for you to be loud.
But when it is unheard, to you,
It cannot be projected.

A false front is unveiled by the uninfected.
Their words of self-projection – they are with
positive hope.
But the veil should never have been lifted.
It cannot be projected.

Serpent

Faith makes serpents
Of those who desire power
Of those who desire wealth
Of those who desire.

Behold as the Lord watches,
Knows your judicial debauchery,
Sees you cast doubt,
Your southpaw assaults,
On all you see about.
For wearing rainbow,
Showing shoulders,
Being prideful and joyous.
Those who wear black,
Sit on church benches,
See the joy of being bound,
Wound up in the strings of
The Church, that

Touches the fresh,
Squeezes the wealth-less,
Clasping the weak
Onto a boat upon waters of
Sin,
"You're free, now".

So say your goodbyes to
the quintessential sinners,
Thou art replaced by the faithful
who claim God's judgement
On their behalf.

Calling

Calling out, reaching out,
Hoping and praying for aid,
Nothing comes, only preaching.
Getting made to think different.

No one to spend time with,
No one to comfort me,
I must upend this life,
Before it makes me conform.

Losing hope, losing grip,
Holding out my hand,
Told I'm wrong, I must have grit,
I can't give in to their demands.
My life is fading with so few hands.
My own hands are raw,
Reaching out in the bitter cold so long,
Test me.
Help me.
I can't look on the bright side,
When my mind and body are this old.

Crawling

My mind shatters,
as your love scatters.
Your life crumbles,
as my happiness stumbles.

Crawling from this ice-cold lake,
I think: was it all fake?
Was it all a lie, or all just broken,
a joke to me, and hope to you?
But who deserved it -
neither of us conserved it,
only soaked it,
drained it and poked it.
A frozen love, desolate.
Empty hole, crumbling.

Seeing you look down,
at my frozen body.
My sodden sorrow, you won't follow.
You borrowed my heart, and can't repair it,
so you stare at me - don't care for me;
hate me and watch me shudder as you close the shutters on me.
Slash me and never come back,
leave me a broken corpse, of broken dreams and endless streams of hope
and
never being able to cope with being left again.
On this icy grass I cry and wallow,
that I didn't ask for this.

I stumble away,
to be humbled,
led astray,
I didn't ask for this,
I didn't want this,
But you did it anyway.

Fight

I couldn't go on.
I cannot go on.
When my fragile bones and fragile mind are so
broken and hollow.
This unbearable weight on my deficient shoulders,
should I follow my heroes?
To take this life from myself isn't stealing,
merely borrowing.
Misery can't be the tether that keeps me here,
fear can't hold my breath.
When I'm so cold and incapable
of keeping up this weeping fight.

So goodnight,
the rain will stop,
no more icy finger,
and no more.
This final wound cannot be healed,
this final noise cannot be heard,
so I follow the path into no man's land.

Careless Suffering

Closer.
A narrow escape from frosted hands,
I feel the shock whisper throughout the
peaks and trenches of my spine.

Empty.
My mind is filled with darkness, silence, pain,
anger and constant careless suffering…
I contemplate, think, wait, alas there is
no hope.
Countless scenarios shoot through
my mind, and never stop.

Cutting.
The pain seeps out of my body,
the pressure built and built,
with no route to escape.
So it filtered through my head,
so it filtered across my knife.
No amount of talking can unleash this
pressure.
I feel, I lose, I give in and
my mind is a minefield,
that I can never stop triggering.

Pain.
Cascading into these aged eyes from this
broken body.
People can tell, people can see, and people
don't care.
Those who I cherish, love, admire,
they do not hear.
they know so many like me.
So, what's the point?

Just one less me.

Kick

Self-destructing,
feeling broken,
seething with hope,
my broken ankles and my foggy mind,
let me be with myself, my own kind,
or I'll collapse from my heels,
the dirt in my feet from digging
my only grave.
Swinging a spade to pierce the ground
as I pierce my life,
my hearse will be on a lonely road,
on the only one-way route from my birth
to my final death.
Kick my tomb,
kick God's womb,
for putting me through this pain.
I cannot continue,
I cannot regain my hope.

Self-Curse

Bleed yourself dry, leech your own limbs,
Eyes so bitter as you cry, pain in your shins.
The tender release of building pressure over
days, weeks, months of pain in dark silence.

Don't love yourself, open the valve,
No more smiles, no more salvation,
Your pipes have burst, your passions evade.
Sit in your corner, drenched in sorrow.

The bright lights will fade, red and blue hue,
It's too late to be saved, you have been you,
They can try and try, but they won't change it.
You can hear them cry, but they won't help you.

Curse yourself, feel the pain drip from you,
as you lose your grip, your body goes numb.
As your hands slip and you feel a shuddering nerve
from your mind to your thumb,
This is the end of your journey, the end of your
trip.

Satin Smile

The Satin Smile of
the man with the beard
the man with the answers

To ease my curious mind
and end my darkest fears
the man who'd never hurt me

The man who stands
before vast tight gates
with a fearsome gait

The man who's plan
involves torture
and sacrifice.

The man who eases minds
through cancer, sickness, death,
who strikes fear in all who hear.

The real tempter,

The real warrior,
Yet I fight his battles

In my mind.
As he stands before
these blackened gates

With a key to his hate
and he opens
and I am told to enter the 'Heavenly' place.

I am not walking on rays
of light, nor rays of sun,
Darkness reigns.

This is no garden of purity
no place of virginity
or sin-free Kingdom.

Temptation from the man
who knows my fate
is blackmail through hate.

The Satin Smile of
the man with hidden horns
and hateful handsome eyes.

The slithering sinner
and his molesting hands
know no bounds of greed

Nor gluttony, love,
this place does not flow
with the songs of Virtue.

The man who makes me
jealous of Endymion,
no punishment is worth this end.

Worth

Am I worth the dirt on my shoe?
Am I worth a cheap rope?
My time is spent alone.
Is there any reason to continue?
Or should I break my own bones?

Am I worth the clinging to sharp relief?
Am I worth the 'tomorrow will be brighter'?
My life is weak.
Is there anything keeping me here?
Or should I just fall into my designated ditch?

Am I worth this?
Am I worth waiting for you?
My return will open the cracks.
Is there anything holding these scars closed?
Or should I open the floodgates?

Worth is assigned by value.
I do not value my life.

Watching the Water

This reflection of my self-hatred burns my eyes,
sets the water alight,
this reflection of my suicide burns my heart,
I can't watch that.
But I can watch the water,
watch myself cry,
watch as I bleed myself dry.
Asking questions but they go unanswered,
asking for directions but it goes unanswered.

This reflection of myself burns me,
sets me alight,
this reflection of my corpse just makes two tragedies,
does not set me apart.
Wicked

This journey does not feel final,
Though I treat myself as a needle in a vinyl,
Scraping out the remaining joy I hold.
I've hit a block in the road,
My life so far is crumbling to dust,
I don't feel like I can continue, though I know I must,
It is such a weight, to carry this load.
Why must I bear this cross?
Does it truly help to emboss my own soul?

I love and it isn't felt,
I hope, though always melt.
I speak and I'm unheard,
I listen, but they don't care.
Am I that wicked?
Or are they that bare?
The effort I expend to want to be loved,
Is it wasted?
Or am I waiting for an impending doom,
Too much in haste?
This wicked life, or my wicked soul?

Who Else?

Who else but you dear?
Speaking so true of love, but no joy.
It is life, I fear,
That ruins all hope,
Neuters us all, I cannot cope, cannot hold.

Without you, who else?
No maiden, nor hope for love that is lost,
It is you, my dear,
You are my cost.
I suffer alone, with noose in my hand

Now I sacrifice,
Fearless, let loose, what vice must keep me here?
Is it you, my love,
That I cannot hear?
Too far, I cannot return, who else
But this empty soul, in this early hearse?

Obsessive

Look at you
so perfect
so pure
so pristine

with your gleaming eyes and
soft sheen
and your glittering
hairs.

Staring through this glass
the reflection
at you
still seeing your perfection.

you are so
perfectly shaped
though never have we spoke
just knowing you
as I do

you are perfect
like a sun in winter
like rain in summer
like my dreams.

Like my head hitting your pillow
after a hard day.
Like me seeing you reflected,
on this rainy window.

Like waking up to see your face,
and never dreaming again,
you are my challenge,
the one for me.

Look at you,
so perfect,
so pure,
but not mine,
only a reflection.

Stranded

The rope I cling to weakens,
threads snap,
this life I wield weighs a ton,
strands are not enough.
For the pain that weakens,
everything I touch.
I'm weighing down
fraying strands.

Let me fall,
let me stop,
let me drop,
no more clinging to broken dreams,
when will these strands die?

No rope can keep me here,
but strands of hope,
I cannot adhere.
You don't keep me here,
I don't hear any pleading,
I only hear my failing strands,
I only hear my bleeding.

Dead Bird

A dead bird,
perched alone on deadwood,
clipped wings,
never flown.

Blood-stained grain,
haunted gliding dreams,
hope for flight,
slaughtered.

A bled-out bird,
on velvet-soaked branches,
decaying in summer light,
never to awake.

Could never soar,
with no clouds to adore,
this dead bird bled free,
yet sits alone and old,
in the wintry cold.

Thank you for reading, this is my first collection, and hopefully not the last. Being 19, it may not be the most mature, or the most perfect poetry, but I am proud to say that I feel as though each poem encapsulates the emotion as I intended.

I would like to thank Freya and Ezra for their support in the publishing of this book, thank you both so much.

Ciarán Lloyd.